Praise for
Expressive Writing for Healing

For more than forty years, I've journaled almost daily. During the months just before and just after my wife's death, journaling was the source of immense relief.

As I read *Expressive Writing for Healing*, I realized I had faced many of the same struggles. It's never over. But life does take on deeper meaning, and we emerge from our grief—different but stronger.

—CECIL MURPHEY, author and coauthor of 140 books, including *90 Minutes in Heaven* with Don Piper; Dr. Ben Carson's autobiography, *Gifted Hands;* and the gift books *When Someone You Love Has Cancer, When Someone You Love No Longer Remembers,* and *Saying Goodbye* with Gary Roe

Mary Potter Kenyon has effectively shared the depths of her heart while gently guiding us through the pain and confusion of grief. As she tells her story, her words give us clear and strong motivation to journal our way through our own stories as we work toward healing. My husband died suddenly nearly twenty years ago, but Mary's words reminded me of the timeless realities of grief that can only be communicated by someone who has been there. You'll find comfort, hope, practical guidance, and inspiration here. I hope you'll open your journal and start writing . . .

—JUDY BRIZENDINE, author of *Stunned By Grief* and *Stunned By Grief Journal*

Mary Potter Kenyon's *Expressive Writing for Healing* is a wonderful book and concept, serving as a road map for the bereaved with wide margins to record the reflections of the journey. Memories of our loved ones do not fade, but recollections of our journey may. This book allows you to document your journey in a meaningful way. William Wordsworth once said, "Poetry is the spontaneous overflow of emotions recollected in tranquility." *Expressive Writing for Healing* allows us to do that: record the poetry from our grieving but hope-filled heart. This book is an inspirational tool for your grief toolbox.

—MITCH CARMODY, author of *Letters to My Son,* highly sought-after speaker for The Compassionate Friends and Tragedy Assistance Program for Survivors (TAPS)

Beautifully written, warm, compassionate, and intensely practical, *Expressive Writing for Healing* was a delight to read and engage with. Mary does a wonderful job of combining her own personal grief experiences and the thoughts of others to guide the reader in expressing and moving through their pain. I only wish I had possessed such a resource during my times of loss.

—GARY ROE, grief counselor and award-winning author of numerous grief books, including *Shattered: Surviving the Loss of a Child, Heartbroken: Healing from the Loss of a Spouse,* and *Please Be Patient, I'm Grieving*

An inspired and amazing resource. In a culture which seeks to avoid pain, Mary Kenyon doesn't show you the way around your heartache, but takes your hand and gently guides you through it. *Expressive Writing for Healing* is the most powerfully framed journal I've ever read. Having lost her mother, husband, and grandson within 17 months of each other, Mary has stitched her soul onto these pages, and then invites you to do the same. This helpful tool is sure to be a welcome companion to the bereaved.

—JOCELYN GREEN, author of *Free to Lean: Making Peace With Your Lopsided Life* and *Faith Deployed: Daily Encouragement for Military Wives*

Mary Potter Kenyon's *Expressive Writing for Healing* provides readers with a beautiful pairing of expertise: the expertise born of her personal experience (Mary lost her mother, husband, and grandson in a three-year period)—and the expertise of a published author and teacher of writing. If loss has come your way, reach for this book early in your grief journey—and learn to capture the words of your loss. By mining Mary's wisdom on the helpful power of journaling, you'll discover a path toward healthy healing for your soul.

—SEPTEMBER VAUDREY, writer and content developer at Willow Creek Community Church, grief workshop presenter, and author of *Colors of Goodbye*

EXPRESSIVE WRITING

for

HEALING

FAMILIUS

Published by Familius LLC, www.familius.com

Familius books are available at special discounts for bulk purchases, whether for sales promotions or for family or corporate use.
For more information, contact Familius Sales at 559-876-2170 or email
orders@familius.com.

Library of Congress Cataloging-in-Publication Data
2017962271

Print ISBN 9781945547447
Ebook ISBN 9781641700276

Printed in the United States of America

Edited by Lindsay Sandberg
Cover design by David Miles
Book design by Brooke Jorden

10 9 8 7 6 5 4 3 2 1

First Edition

EXPRESSIVE WRITING

for

HEALING

Journal Your Way

From Grief to Hope

MARY POTTER KENYON

Dedicated to Byron and Irma Potter,
David Kenyon, and my beautiful
grandson, Jacob Flesher.

CONTENTS

FOREWORD

What's the value in journaling? This is a question I asked myself for years. It wasn't until my sister was diagnosed with cancer that I fully understood and appreciated the art of writing about one's day in a diary.

When my sister was diagnosed with aggressive stage-four breast cancer at age thirty-six, doctors also discovered that she was newly pregnant. Her prognosis was grim. With two young daughters at home, we were certain she would agree to a pregnancy termination and begin aggressive, lifesaving treatment.

But she didn't consent.

She flat out refused.

She couldn't bring herself to terminate the precious life growing inside her womb, even if it meant certain death for herself.

And thus began the next chapter in our family's lives as we watched, prayed, and waited for a miracle.

All through that time, my sister wrote in her journal. She had kept journals for years, storing them in neat piles in her bedroom closet. But now, the journals represented something else—a heartfelt explanation to her two young daughters. One day, when they were old enough to understand, they would inherit their mother's journals and learn why she had made the decisions she had.

But for now, the journals were my sister's secret place to pour out her feelings, her fears, and her prayers for a miracle.

"We do not know the true value of our moments until they have undergone the test of memory." —Georges Duhamel

And this is when I developed an appreciation for keeping a journal—because had she died, my sister's journals would have been a lifeline to her memory.

Like my sister, Mary Potter Kenyon is a prolific writer, and a skilled one at that. Much of her writing draws upon her own diary and allows us an intimate glimpse inside her world. It's a world full of challenges, loss, and heartbreak. But it's also a world that's rich in love, beauty, and gems of wisdom born from her experiences.

In *Expressive Writing for Healing*, Mary has crafted a gem of a guidebook for anyone interested in the art of journal-keeping. She doesn't just tell us how to journal; she expertly guides us with love, direction, and snippets of wisdom in the form of essays. There is no better teacher about how to journal through loss than Mary herself.

Allow Mary to be your guide as you put pen to paper and pour out your feelings and fears. As you embark on a journey of self-discovery, the journal becomes the keeper of your pain, your anger, your questions, and your hopes. And your love. It becomes a secret haven that's safe from judgment, criticism, and English teachers.

"I don't want to live in a hand-me-down world of others' experiences. I want to write about me, my discoveries, my fears, my feelings, about me." —Helen Keller

Go ahead—take that leap to begin writing down your thoughts, feelings, and reactions to life experiences. With Mary Potter Kenyon by your side, once you begin, you'll be able to look back and move forward without fear.

Lynda Cheldelin Fell
Publisher, Grief Diaries series
www.Lyndafell.com

INTRODUCTION

The morning after my husband, David, died, I pulled out a personalized journal from the cabinet where I'd stashed it several months before. The photo on the cover was one of us together, along with the words "Grow old along with me." When I'd ordered it with a special discount coupon code, I wasn't sure what I was going to do with it. Several coupon codes later, I'd collected other journals, a similarly personalized tote bag, a set of notecards, and even postage stamps emblazoned with our happy faces and the "grow old along with me" sentiment. The words made famous by poet Robert Browning held special meaning for me. David had survived a cancer experience that had dramatically improved our marriage. We were the happiest we'd ever been, and I treasured our newly revitalized relationship, looking forward to many more years together.

But there would be no growing old together. David unexpectedly passed away three days after coming home from the hospital following a heart stent surgery in March 2012. It was the day before his sixty-first birthday. I was fifty-two years old, and the youngest of our eight children would turn nine that summer.

The notecards went into the trash bin. The tote was filled with sympathy cards and shoved into a trunk, where it remains to this day. I used the personalized postage stamps to send out thank-you notes after David's funeral. And the journals? Forty-eight hours after my spouse's death, I sat at my kitchen table and wrote down all the things I was grateful for: the bonus five and a half years with my husband after his cancer, our revitalized relationship, my eight children, the siblings who surrounded me like cotton batting, and my husband's life insurance policy that had been reinstated just twenty-seven days before.

I filled three pages that morning and, in the ensuing months, the entire journal. I began another one. In that first year of grieving, I filled two journals and started on a third. A writer by trade, it seemed only natural to choose writing as my therapy. Sometimes, even now, I flip through the pages of those first journals, and though it hurts to revisit the extraordinary pain I was experiencing, I can see how the act of writing my way through grief may have saved me.

Looking back through that first journal, I see something else. It's clear how much better I was doing by the time I'd filled it. Those journals are an affirmation that growth and healing were taking place.

EXPRESSIVE WRITING 101

The first "rule" for this journal is that there are no rules. This book is designed with empty pages to be utilized however you want. It's meant to be a safe place for expressing your thoughts, emotions, desires, and dreams, and if that means filling some of the empty space with doodles or drawings, composing poetry, using scrapbook materials for personalization, or the standard of freewriting one usually associates with a journal, feel free to engage in whatever method of self-expression comes naturally. Everyone expresses themselves differently, and sometimes, simple words might not be able to hold all of the emotions you are experiencing during your grief journey. Find your healing expression. Paint. Write. Gather pictures. Write a song. A friend of mine glues or tapes cards, notes, or meaningful memorabilia into her journal, and that's perfectly acceptable too.

That said, you will want to incorporate some freewriting into your use of this journal. Notice that I use the term "freewriting." That means you are free to write whatever you want, in any way. Don't worry about grammar, proper syntax, or neat handwriting. While there is no right or wrong way to utilize a journal, there's a body of science behind utilizing expressive writing as a healing tool.

Dr. James Pennebaker, Regents Centennial Chair of Psychology at the University of Texas in Austin, is a pioneer in the study of using expressive writing as a route to healing. His research has shown that short-term focused writing can have a beneficial effect for anyone dealing with stress and trauma. In a late-1980s study with his students, participants in the experimental group were instructed to write their deepest feelings and thoughts about a past trauma or emotional upheaval, while those in a control group were instructed to write on a neutral topic. Pennebaker and his colleague, Sandra Beall, were initially discouraged when the writing caused distress among the group of students, with some crying, and others reporting a feeling of sadness. Four months later, however, the participants in the experimental group reported a significant lift in their spirits. Six months after the experiment, those who had written about their distressing experience showed marked improvement in immune-system function and had fewer visits to the health center.

In his book *Opening Up: The Healing Power of Confiding in Others*, Pennebaker summarized ten years of scientific research into the connection between opening up about emotionally difficult or traumatic events and the positive changes in brain and immune function. He concluded that it isn't the simple act of writing alone that promotes healing in the emotionally wounded. Instead, it is reflection and searching for meaning in the experiences that has proven helpful.

Since then, Pennebaker's original expressive-writing paradigm has been replicated in hundreds of studies, each measuring different potential effects of expressive writing.

Not only has subsequent research confirmed Pennebaker's original finding regarding physical well-being, but writing about emotionally charged topics has been shown to improve mental health, reducing symptoms of depression or anxiety. This has proven true in studies with veterans experiencing PTSD, cancer patients, and those who have experienced a loss of some sort, including a job.

In one of Pennebaker's studies, fifty middle-aged professionals who were terminated from a large Dallas computer company were split into two groups. The first group wrote for thirty minutes a day, five days in a row, about their personal experience of being fired. The second group wrote for the same period of time on an unrelated topic. Within three months, 27 percent of the expressive writers had landed jobs, compared with less than 5 percent of the participants in the control group.

While I reiterate that there are no rules in how to utilize this journal, as you share the stirrings of your heart and the aches of your soul, I offer this gentle guidance:

Give yourself quiet, contemplative time.

I realize how difficult it can be to sit quietly after a loss. If you are a parent and have children living with you, if you work full-time, or if you've simply been avoiding being alone because you're afraid you'll go stark raving mad in quiet isolation, realize that we cannot run from our loss. It will catch up with us. Nor should we continue to keep so busy that we aren't allowing ourselves the quiet time that is essential to healing.

In his original research, Pennebaker had his subjects write for fifteen minutes a day, four days in a row. Later studies included twenty minutes for four days. Try setting a similar pattern. In her book, *The Artist's Way*, author and creativity guru Julia Cameron claims the secret to productivity and getting rid of the clutter in your brain is to master the practice of "Morning Pages," filling three blank pages of a journal or notebook every day.

Find what works for you, whether it is ten minutes every morning or half an hour on Saturday and Sunday. During my husband's cancer treatment in 2006, I wrote daily while he was in the hospital after his surgery. After he was released, I wrote sporadically throughout the week, but consistently on Wednesdays during his chemotherapy treatments. I'd sit next to him, holding his hand with my free hand while I wrote with the other. Instinctively, I wrote daily for several months after his death, wondering how anyone could get through such trauma without writing about it. Now, I might journal once a week or more often when I'm working through something.

Don't censor yourself or hold back.

This journal is for *you*. Don't worry about someone else reading your words, at least for now. If it helps to think that you will dispose of the journal later, feel free to consider doing so if that frees you to write from the heart. Someday, you might burn it or tear pages out. Personally, I've made the decision to leave my journals intact so that when one of my children inevitably faces the loss of a loved one, they'll be able to read my journals and realize that not only did their mom survive as a widow but she also eventually thrived.

When my husband died, one of the first people I longed to communicate with was my mother. She was the only widow I knew, but she'd passed away just seventeen months before. How wonderful it would have been to be able to read a chronicle of her words regarding how she dealt with the loss of my father. I have pieces of that in a memory book she left behind, but I would have liked more.

Whatever you end up doing with this book, keep in mind that the writing is for you and not an audience. You can't help yourself if you're holding back and not being honest about what you're feeling. Grief is messy, so it's perfectly fine if your journal is too. When I began writing in a journal after my husband's death, I didn't know that sections of my journal would eventually make their way into a book chronicling the triple whammy of mother, husband, and grandson loss I experienced in the space of three years, but I was certainly glad for the access I had to those journal entries and the immediacy of those memories.

Write down your dreams, both figurative and literal.

The death of a loved one can throw your life into turmoil, drastically affecting planned life and day-to-day activities. It's natural to wonder what the rest of your life will look like without that person. Did you have dreams and desires for your future? How have they changed? What do you want for yourself now? Write it all down. In a couple of years, you may look back and see some of those dreams have become reality. In my case, my husband dreamed lofty goals for me: book publication and public speaking. Because he believed in me, I dared to write those goals in my journal after his death, feeling his approval when they were met.

Our subconscious also works hard to process significant changes. Have you had any particularly vivid nighttime dreams since the loss of your loved one? Write those down too. I've experienced several dreams about David where I could feel his arms around me or hear his voice, and I would wake up feeling as though he'd actually visited with me. More than once, I've woken up from a dream, my face wet with tears. While I didn't remember the dream that had caused the tears, once I was fully awake I realized the significance of the date—often an anniversary of some sort.

If you are reading, jot down passages or quotes that inspire you.

The quotes found on these pages are ones I copied down in my journal as I worked my way through the early days of bereavement. I didn't fill those first two journals just with my own ranting and raving. I was reading voraciously: Max Lucado devotionals, the Bible, and dozens of books by authors who had gone down the path of grief before me. When I read something particularly inspiring or uplifting that resonated with me, I jotted those passages or quotes down in my journal. I've often referred to those journals in the ensuing years and can still find inspiration and encouragement from the words I chose to transcribe.

If you pick up a book and begin reading but don't feel encouraged or uplifted, I give you permission to just stop reading. There are too many good books out there to waste your time with one that isn't lifting you in some way, even if it is to laugh out loud, like I did when I read Lolly Winston's fictional *Good Grief*.

Grief is a heavy weight to carry. Grieving is exhausting. If a quote included on one of these pages encourages you and you want to refer to that author's book, all the titles are included in the resource section at the back.

If someone sends you a particularly poignant letter or note, consider stashing it in your journal. For me, it was some notebook pages full of Bible verses a young woman had copied down and sent me; an encouraging note; and a couple of pages torn from a Max Lucado book. Yes, librarian Mary destroyed an entire (garage sale) book to salvage the section that spoke to her. I transferred those loose pages to my second journal once I had filled the first.

Date your journal entries, attempting to end them in a positive way.

Did something good happen today? Can you find something to be grateful for? By ending your journal entry on a positive note—with a note of gratitude or perhaps a prayer—you are training yourself to consciously choose joy and gratitude even in the midst of pain. Yes, *joy*. Because you will feel joy again. In the beginning of your grief journey, you might only see glimpses of it, but hold on to those tiny bursts of light, noting them in your journal. Those are pieces of hope.

It might not be easy, but there's always something to be thankful for, even if it is a smile from a stranger in the grocery store.

Feel free to utilize the writing prompts at the end of the journal.

For those who aren't used to writing down their thoughts, there are optional writing prompts listed before the resource section. I purposely avoided designing this as a guided journal, because I personally resist being told what to write. But the same might not be true for you. Maybe an assigned topic is all it takes to jumpstart your expressive writing some mornings.

We do not write in order to be understood;
we write in order to understand.
—C. Day-Lewis

Writing is not only a reflection of what one
thinks and feels, but a rope one weaves with
words that can lower you below or hoist you
above the surface of your life, enabling you to go
deeper or higher than you would otherwise go.
—Phyllis Theroux, *The Journal Keeper*

> People who write about their loved one's deaths are paradoxically engaged in a search for the meaning of their loved one's lives. They want to make a record; they want to describe their loss and their grief. But they want to discover, too, an overarching meaning for this death so that it will not have been for naught.
>
> —Louise DeSalvo, *Writing as a Way of Healing*

In fact, finding my way is why I took up journal-keeping in the first place. I was, to paraphrase Dante, in the middle of a dark wood. My journal was a flashlight. It still is.
—Phyllis Theroux, *The Journal Keeper*

IN THE BEGINNING

I kept repeating the details of that morning over and over to anyone who'd listen. I'd note the shock that mirrored my own in the listener's expression as I'd relate how I'd settled on the couch next to the chair where my husband sat with his eyes closed, the remote control in his hand. I drank a cup of coffee while I penned a letter to my friend Mary. For at least half an hour, maybe more, I contentedly drank from my mug and wrote, muted voices from the television in the background, while the house silently awaited the discovery.

"How could I not have known?" I asked.

David had survived cancer five years before. He had survived a heart attack and stent surgery, and had come home from the hospital. I'd left him in the chair the night before when I'd gone up to bed. Had I even kissed him goodnight? I couldn't remember, couldn't even dredge up the memory of our last shared kiss from the deep recesses of my mind.

How could I not have known? How could I have loved someone so much and not have sensed immediately that he was gone?

What came next, I did not share as readily: the noise from deep in my throat, the frantic call to 911, the words that came jumbled from my mouth, the man who suddenly appeared at my door, and then, another. I cannot tell you how many people were suddenly in my house or what they looked like, but I do know that at some point, my husband's body was on the floor, emergency responders working over him. I couldn't bear to watch their fruitless resuscitation efforts. I ran up the steps to change from my pajamas. I cannot say if I first pulled on clothes or woke sixteen-year-old Emily, or which one of us woke eighteen-year-old Matt. The three of us were standing at the bottom of the stairs when twelve-year-old Katie woke up from the commotion. Eight-year-old Abby remained asleep.

I know Emily ran across the street to her older brother Dan's door, and they stood on his porch, watching as their father was loaded into an ambulance. Matt drove me to the hospital, stopping at his sister Elizabeth's house on the way, where my son-in-law, Ben, met me at the door. David had been Ben's friend, as well as his father-in-law. I registered horror on his face as he promised to wake Elizabeth.

There were two more children to reach, two more calls to make, but I don't remember how or when those calls were made. I only know that my six oldest children and I ended up in a small room with a priest and a social worker, while Katie and Abby were left behind at home with my sister Denise. I must have called her to come stay with them, but I don't remember that, either.

Katie, awake when the rest of us left, must have known her dad was gone before we returned home to confirm it. Today, my heart aches to realize she was alone at the house while Denise took Abby to the store for cereal as a diversion from the truth she couldn't be the one to tell. I'll never forget the look on Abby's face as her body shook with sobs when I informed her that Daddy had died sometime in the night.

I couldn't reach anyone in David's family at their homes, so I had to call his sister Susan at work. I remember asking her if she was sitting down—the stock question always heard in movies and books—before I blurted out the news.

Shock numbed the pain as my own sisters bustled around the house, folding laundry, doing dishes, maybe feeding us. Certainly, we must have eaten something. And there I sat, repeating the details over and over, until night set in and I collapsed in exhaustion on the couch. Four of my daughters joined me, and we slept fitfully in the living room two nights in a row, maybe three.

Writing was the way I worked through everything. It's how I got through my husband's cancer in 2006 and my mother's death in 2010. Of course, I would be the one to write the obituary for my beloved. The morning after his death, my fingers thick with grief, I struggled to move pen across paper. The next day, March 29, 2012, I pulled out a journal and filled three pages with all I was thankful for.

By March 31, I was sleeping on a mattress on the floor of the room of my two youngest daughters. I know this because I wrote it down in my journal. I'd get up each morning, make coffee, sit at the kitchen table, and write. During those early days, each morning brought fresh loss, the realization as I got out of bed and walked down the stairs: David is gone.

I also know that I went to the doctor on April 2 for medication for anxiety, because that is noted in my journal—just as, a year later, I jotted down that the pill bottle had remained untouched in my cupboard.

I wrote about the extreme exhaustion I was experiencing, the brain fog, and my worries about returning to the workshops I'd been teaching.

Because I kept a journal, I marked April 3 as the first "good" day since my husband's death. I'd functioned, going to the grocery store and the post office. I know that on the morning of April 10, daily visits from my sisters ceased. When I'd realized no one was coming that day, I'd leaned over the back of the couch, pushed aside the curtains of the front window, and searched the street, tears streaming down my face. I'd never felt more alone. My sisters had to return to their regularly scheduled days, but my life had been irrevocably changed.

I know all these things because I wrote about them, searching for meaning in my loss. I also know that by the time I filled that first journal in October, seven months after my husband's death, I was having more good days than bad—at least until the first holidays hit.

I write of these things now because some memories of our early grieving remain indelible in our minds, while others are murky. Until my friend Mary gave me back the letter I'd written her that fateful morning, I'd believed I'd gotten up from the couch to wake David for his coffee. Instead, the letter reminded me that I had been going to wake him up to tell him something I'd forgotten to say the night before. I cannot count the number of times since then that I've wanted to do the same thing: tell him something.

Mostly, I've wanted to share what it is to live without him.

Now I am setting out into the unknown.
It will take me a long while to work
through the grief. There are no
shortcuts; it has to be gone through.
—Madeleine L'Engle, *Two-Part Invention*

My soul sighs a lot these days. I'm tired
all the time. Even thinking is a chore.
—Gary Roe, *Please Be Patient, I'm Grieving*

Many of us are tempted to think that if we suffer, the only important thing is to be relieved of our pain. We want to flee it at all costs. But when we learn to move through suffering, rather than avoid it, then we greet it differently. We become willing to let it teach us. We even begin to see how God can use it for some larger end.

—Henri Nouwen, *Turn My Mourning into Dancing*

Grief is beyond understanding to those who
have not received a personal introduction.
—Judy Brizendine, *Stunned By Grief*

MARKING TIME

Certain moments from that morning and the days following March 27, 2012, are etched in my brain: the moment I touched my husband's chest and called out his name; the moan that escaped in a voice I didn't recognize as my own when I realized he was gone; my youngest child's face and her sobs when I told her. I can recall each of these details with an eerie clarity.

Time stopped, figuratively and literally, the day my husband died. Both the kitchen clock and the one in my office inexplicably ceased working that morning. I wish now I had paid attention to the hour they stopped. Was it the minute, the very moment that my husband had died?

Instead, I was too numb to wonder at the coincidence. Time had no meaning for me. It was visitors who noticed neither clock was working; *I* certainly didn't care. During those first few days, I measured time by the daylight, automatically rising when the sun rose and falling into bed shortly after it set.

When time resumed, it ticked away slowly. I'd get up, open the front door, make a cup of coffee, and sit at the table, leaving the door wide open. My sisters wouldn't even knock; they'd walk in to find me in the kitchen or on the couch, writing in my journal. When they'd point out that the clocks still weren't working, I'd just shrug my shoulders. What difference did it make?

I felt as though I was moving underwater. I'd rise from bed, get dressed, sit at the table with a cup of coffee, and write. Sometimes, I didn't even bother to get dressed. Then I'd go to the couch, where a pile of notebooks and books surrounded me. The books would change. Pages filled with writing. For weeks, the piles remained, until my children began referring to that section of the couch as "Mom's nest."

I'm lucky to have had the luxury of not needing to do anything or go anywhere—outside of a wake and funeral— for three weeks after David's death. I wasn't sure how I'd go back to conducting the couponing and writing workshops I was scheduled for. David had been such a big part of them, accompanying me whenever he could.

My first visit to the grocery store was a disaster. I left my partially filled cart in the peanut butter aisle and bolted to my car, where I cried in anguish, slamming my fists against the steering wheel. David had loved peanut butter.

How do people do this? I wondered then—and still wonder today when I meet someone recently bereaved out in public.

You're walking around? Conducting business and running errands? I refrain from marveling out loud, knowing so few of the wounded have any choice in the matter. My son-in-law, Ben, was allotted three days off work after his son died. Three days.

Time marched on, and I was expected to do the same. Someone eventually replaced the batteries of the clocks. Three weeks after my husband's death, I survived my first workshop, even managing to crack a joke or two during it. The next workshop was easier. During my second shopping trip, I avoided one aisle but otherwise got all the way through the grocery store, checking out without incident.

I'm grateful for the months I had before I needed to find employment. I wrote and read my way through much of those early weeks of bereavement. It seems odd to say now that I miss the unhurried pace of that period of time, but I do. Though it isn't likely I would have experienced it without loss, the slowness of those days was a gift, a balm to a wounded soul.

Time has no meaning during early mourning. The griever might lose track of time, even forgetting what day it is. At my husband's funeral luncheon, our priest and the servers weren't eating the delicious meal I'd chosen, and I wondered why. When someone commented that it was humorous that I'd ordered roast beef to be served on a Friday during Lent, I looked at them blankly. *Is it Lent?* I wondered. *Is it Friday?*

Whether or not you have time off before you have to resume daily responsibilities, while the grief is fresh, time isn't measured like it was before. Dating and recording events in a journal will help you keep track of the days. Looking back at those early entries can be healing after the fog lifts.

Sadness helps us make these kinds of adjustments by giving us a forced "timeout." . . . Sadness slows us down and, by doing so, seems to slow the world down. Sometimes bereaved people even say that living with the sadness of loss is like living in slow motion. There seems to be less need to pay attention to the world around us, so we are able to put aside normal, everyday concerns and to turn our attention inward.

—George A. Bonanno, *The Other Side of Sadness*

_____

_____

_____

_____

_____

_____

_____

_____

_____

_____

_____

_____

_____

_____

_____

_____

_____

_____

_____

_____

_____

_____

_____

_____

Everything is different now, including our sense of
time. Grief and loss are like some weird alternate
universe. The whole experience is surreal.
—Gary Roe, *Heartbroken*

We can run from the darkness, or we can
enter into the darkness and face the pain
of loss. We can indulge ourselves in self-
pity, or we can empathize with others and
embrace their pain as our own. We can run
away from sorrow and drown it in addictions,
or we can learn to live with sorrow.
—Jerry L. Sittser, *A Grace Disguised:
How the Soul Grows through Loss*

At other times, it feels like being mildly
drunk, or concussed. There is a sort of
invisible blanket between the world and me.
I find it hard to take in what anyone says.
—C. S. Lewis, *A Grief Observed*

FAILING AT GRIEF

66 **I** can't even do this right," I reflected early on in grieving my husband. My mother had lost so much weight after my dad died, we'd worried we were going to lose her too. I initially lost weight after David's death but gained it back, and then some. If losing drastic amounts of weight was the measure of true sorrow, I was failing at grief.

There was no handbook on grieving. I'd wonder if I was doing it wrong, as if there were a prescribed way to grieve. So many of the articles and books I read about bereavement referred to Elisabeth Kübler-Ross and the "five stages" of grief. Because of that, I expected mourning to be somewhat linear in progression. I was dismayed, then, when it wasn't. I experienced no real sense of denial beyond those first hours—and never any anger. Who would I have been angry at? Certainly not God, who'd given me David in the first place, and never at the man who hadn't wanted to leave me or his children.

Not only that, but much to the dismay of my three youngest daughters, I wanted to talk about my loss all the time, even to strangers in the grocery store. And while my girls didn't mind when I talked to them about their father, they made it clear I wasn't to mention "Dad's death" in front of their friends, even though the friends were well aware of the situation.

"Why do you always have to bring up Dad in public?" one of them lamented after overhearing yet another conversation with someone I didn't know well.

Tears stung my eyes, and I choked up with emotion as I attempted to explain that after nearly thirty-five years together, I couldn't bear not talking about him. He remained a huge part of my life. After that, the girls stopped questioning my method of grieving, but that didn't mean they liked it.

My two younger sons didn't talk much about the loss, though their older brother, Dan, openly grieved, as did my two oldest daughters. Not one of my eight children, however, felt the need to share with strangers or coworkers, and my oldest daughter, Elizabeth, barely had the chance to grieve her dad in any way at all. The day after his funeral, she was in the hospital with her six-year-old son, Jacob. His cancer had returned, and he faced months of treatment, his mother by his side at all times.

In January 2013, less than a year after David's death, we were informed that Jacob's cancer was terminal. When he died in August, two months after his eighth birthday, there was nothing I could do or say to alleviate the anguish of my daughter and son-in-law, Ben. I couldn't even hold my daughter to comfort her. Elizabeth wasn't a hugger; she'd stiffen in response to any attempt to console her with physical contact. There was certainly no handbook for this.

How does one grieve a child?

A Compassionate Friends support group was an option, but neither Elizabeth nor Ben were interested in attending one. We stumbled blindly through the first year, my heart aching for them.

When Elizabeth asked me to attend The Compassionate Friends national conference in Dallas, Texas, in 2015, I readily agreed, even though it would have made more sense for *her* to go. I'd have done anything she asked if I thought it would help her in some way.

"I want you to go and speak to the hearts of grieving mothers," she insisted. By then, I was already speaking on finding hope in the darkness of grief.

There were grieving grandparents in attendance, but it wasn't to them I gravitated. Instead, I'd scan the rooms for young women my daughter's age and sit near them. I'd lean forward at the lunch table to listen to their conversations, gleaning insight into what it was to lose a child. Fathers grieved differently, I gathered. And the loss of a child, which is certainly a challenge to marriage, didn't mean an inevitable divorce.

No two stories of loss and grief were the same. I heard anger, blame, and guilt in their stories, but it was the tales of hope and faith I held close to my heart. I knew from attending many workshops that there was no right or wrong way to grieve. I grasped a young stranger's hands when she asked me to pray for her in a hallway and hugged another close to me as she cried in the bathroom, ministering to these grieving mothers as if they were my own daughter.

At the beginning of my own presentation, I admitted that I didn't know the particular loss of a child—that I didn't know how to take their pain away from them any more than I could take it from my daughter.

"But I lost something besides a grandson the day Jacob died," I told the room of grief-stricken parents. "I lost the ability to help my child, to make it better—because nothing will take the pain of losing a child away."

I saw tears in the eyes of an older woman sitting next to a younger version of herself.

"If you have someone in your life who loves you like that," I added, "someone who wants to help, let them try. You lost your child. They don't want to lose theirs."

With that, the older woman took the hand of the younger one, who didn't pull away. Both of them were openly crying.

I knew then: I couldn't walk the path of child loss for my daughter. It was hers to walk alone and on her own terms. Even if I couldn't hug her or hold her hand, she knew I was there for her.

A year later, I heard David Kessler, a colleague of Elisabeth Kübler-Ross, speak. He stated that the five stages of grief have evolved since they were introduced and have been very misunderstood over the past three decades.

They were never meant to help tuck messy emotions into neat packages. They are responses to loss that many people have, but there is not a typical response to loss, as there is no typical loss. Our grief is as individual as our lives. . . . The five stages—denial, anger, bargaining, depression, and acceptance—are a part of the framework that makes up our learning to live with the one we lost. They are tools to help us frame and identify what we may be feeling. But they are not stops on some linear timeline in grief. Not everyone goes through all of them or goes in a prescribed order. (Kessler and Kübler-Ross, Grief & Grieving: Finding the Meaning of Grief Through the Five Stages of Loss*)*

My incessant need to talk about the loss, as well as my daughters' desire not to, was normal—for us. One son's innate ability to listen and another one's avoidance of the topic—all perfectly fine. Elizabeth's resistance of hugs and hand-holding was just part of her personality.

Your journal is a safe place to sort through all that mess. To write what you can't say. No censure. No right or wrong. Whether you need to rant, lament, deny, bargain, beg, pray, or express gratitude, your journal can handle it. It will hold anything you throw at it and help relieve some of the emotional burden.

There is no one way to grieve, no prescribed steps in mourning. No pass or fail. No grades. I hadn't been failing at grief; I'd simply been grieving in my own way.

Grief is the least linear thing I know. Hardly
a tidy progression of stages, grief tends
to be unruly. It works with the most raw
and elemental forces in us, which makes it
unpredictable and wild. Grief resists our attempts
to force it along a prescribed path. It propels
us in directions we had not planned to go.
—Jan Richardson, *The Cure for Sorrow:*
A Book of Blessings for Times of Grief

Be open to how God wants to work
for your good. He can use *everything* in
our lives—even the greatest tragedy or
pain—to bring about something good.
—Judy Brizendine, *Stunned By Grief*

One day you are acting almost like a normal person. You maybe even manage to take a shower. Your clothes match. You think the autumn leaves look pretty, or enjoy the sound of snow crunching under your feet.

—Ann Hood, *Comfort: A Journey Through Grief*

I entered the afterloss broken and shattered.
It's like I had this big bag of fragments I once
called life and dumped them in the middle
of this new world and said, "Here. This is
all I've got left. What can I do with this?"
—Benjamin Allen, *Out of the Ashes*

DON'T CRY FOR ME

Approximately four months after David died, I was carrying a basket of laundry down the basement stairs when it suddenly dawned on me that I hadn't cried for more than twenty-four hours, not even a sob in the darkness of night. I stood stock-still on the landing, the basket sliding from my hands, splaying dirty laundry all over the steps. Then, I sat down and started crying because I never wanted to forget David.

I shook my head at the incongruity of crying about not crying.

Not quite two years later, I was sitting in a dentist's chair when the hygienist asked me what was going on in my life—and why I hadn't been taking care of my teeth. I started to explain how oral hygiene had been the last thing on my mind since losing my mother, husband, and grandson in the space of three years, when I realized tears were streaming down my cheeks. Suddenly, I was sobbing uncontrollably.

Horrified, I attempted to stem the flow of tears but to no avail. The bewildered young woman handed me a tissue and bolted out of the room. It took me several minutes to regain my composure.

In his book, *Understanding Your Grief: Ten Essential Touchstones for Finding Hope and Healing Your Heart*, Dr. Alan D. Wolfelt calls episodes like these "griefbursts," when a person is overcome with a sudden, overwhelming sense of missing the person they loved and will begin crying openly, even sobbing.

We can't always predict when a wave of grief will assail us. Why shouldn't we allow ourselves tears when it does? Science has proven that crying is cathartic and can be good for us. According to Purnendu Ghosh in his book, *Neural Suitcase Tells the Tales of Many Minds*, emotional tears contain higher levels of the adrenocorticotropic hormone prolactin (a stress hormone), the painkiller leucine enkephalin, and manganese, which helps regulate mood. Chronically depressed people often have high levels of manganese in their systems. A good cry can release the excess hormones that cause physical ailments and mood disorders. Thanks to the chemicals leaving the body, those who are grieving can relieve stress and feel more relaxed through crying.

When I first began doing presentations for grief support groups, I wasn't sure what to do when attendees who approached me afterward began crying. Initially, I thought it imperative to help them stem the flow of their tears at all costs. After all, the person was obviously embarrassed, trying to do the same thing with the tissues they kept balled up in their fists. At some point, however, I started setting out tissue packets beforehand and took the time to explain that crying is a healthy response to grief. I always remind attendees that everyone in the room is there for the same reason, and it's a safe place to display their emotion. Essentially, I give them permission to cry. I've learned to welcome the tears, to sit quietly, and to offer companionship through loss.

When a wave of grief hits, feel free to pour it out in writing, without censoring or stifling the emotions that emerge. Notice if the emotion was triggered by an anniversary or milestone, a dream, a memory, or the unearthing of forgotten mementos. And as the griefburst washes over you, recognize that this outpouring of grief is an indication of how much you loved.

Deep love brings deep grief. The only way to avoid grief completely would be to not become emotionally attached to anyone. Loving my husband was worth the resulting pain upon the loss of him. How many of us would give up the experience of having loved, just to avoid grief?

Between grief and nothing, I will take grief.
—William Faulkner

There is a sacredness in tears. They are not the
mark of weakness, but of power. They speak
more eloquently than ten thousand tongues.
They are the messengers of overwhelming grief,
of deep contrition, and of unspeakable love.
—Washington Irving

Still, if we want to avoid the suffering of leaving, we will never experience the joy of loving. And love is stronger than fear, life stronger than death, hope stronger than despair. We have to trust that the risk of loving is always worth taking.

—Henri Nouwen

Ignore the need to be "strong." Tears are
a gift, and they often demonstrate how
precious our loved one was to us.
—Shelly Beach

BE STILL

For weeks after David's death, I wrote voraciously. Every single morning, I'd get up, make coffee, plop down on the couch, pick up my pen, and begin writing, strains of Kenny G or the Christian radio station playing in the background. I wrote articles, essays, blog entries, and letters, and I worked on a book that David had encouraged me to write. But while writing served as a therapeutic tool for me, it also became a way to avoid confronting my loss. As long as I was frantically writing, I was keeping my mind too busy to fully contemplate what I'd lost. I was running away in my mind just as surely as another widow I met was running away in an RV. For the first year after her husband's death, she and her homeschooled children traveled the country. When they finally parked the RV in their own driveway, she fell apart.

"It hit me hard then that Doug was never coming back to us," she told me. "I finally faced my grief, and it nearly did me in."

When I wasn't writing, I was reading: devotionals, the Bible, books by authors who had been down the road of grief before me, and on the science of bereavement. Even as I read, music played in the background. I couldn't stand silence, because it was in the still, quiet moments that I'd break down. If I forgot to turn on the radio when I was alone in the vehicle, I'd inevitably need to pull over to the side of the road when I couldn't see through my tears. I avoided contemplative silence at all costs.

So, when I got up one morning and couldn't write, I panicked. I turned up the music, thinking it would surely inspire me. I squirmed when the words still did not come. I got up from the couch and paced back and forth, then sat back down to try again, to no avail. My heart raced. I couldn't breathe. This went on for several days. Each time I'd attempt to write, I'd hear "be still," and I'd balk. I wanted none of that. I knew what happened when I allowed myself quiet time.

I don't know who gave me the book or what possessed me to pick up Martha Beck's *The Joy Diet* during those days. Maybe it was a gift from someone who wanted to see me joyful again. Maybe I'd gotten it for myself, wishing the same thing. Whatever the case, when I read these words, I knew I needed to pay attention:

> *If you have suffered greatly and not yet resolved your pain, you may find it literally unbearable to become physically still; the moment you really quiet your body, you'll feel the monsters of unprocessed grief, rage, or fear yammering at the dungeon doors of your subconscious mind. This can trigger an intense fight/flight reaction, flooding your body with adrenaline that will render you angry, anxious, or restless, rather than peaceful.*

Beck suggested trying short bursts of stillness, easing into longer periods of quiet, contemplative solitude. I knew I needed to try it if I wanted my writing ability back. So I turned off the radio, read from a devotional, and then attempted to sit still, to just "be." The pain hit, *hard*. I wanted to run from it. Instead, I leaned in, letting myself experience the searing pain that would rise and then gradually ebb.

I learned the truth of what Beck went on to say:

Almost all of us have been assaulted by hurricane winds, rapacious fires, and shattering earthquakes of some sort; we live on that kind of planet. Do you remember the last time your preconceptions were blown to smithereens, your heart burnt to a cinder, your confidence shattered? Look back on it now (or if you're in the middle of it, look around) and see if in the midst of that devastation—right in the center of it—you half-sense something still and small. Listen for it. Beneath, around, even within the cacophonous chaos of your life disintegrating, something infinitely powerful and surpassingly sweet is whispering to you. It is when all our somethings are collapsing that we may finally turn to nothing, and find there everything we need.

Whenever I allowed for contemplative silence, I was assaulted by the painful acknowledgement of my incredible loss. But I needed to face it, to actively mourn. All the writing in the world wasn't going to keep David alive or bring him back.

In the midst of that terrible darkness, I did indeed catch glimpses of light—little pinpricks in the dark. And for the first time in my life, by forcing myself to "be still," I was learning what it was to listen. I didn't just call out to God in anguish. I could discern the still, small voice telling me I was not alone, that I would be okay.

In those quiet moments—once the waves of pain receded, and I was left with a manageable dull ache—I discerned whispers of hope. Others had gone down this path before me, and they'd survived. My own mother had, living alone more than twenty-five years after my dad's death. Authors of the grief memoirs I was reading had not only survived, but they'd also lived to write about it.

At the same time, through practicing stillness, my senses were heightened. Instead of rushing everywhere, I consciously slowed down. The fog of grief lifted slightly, and as if for the first time, I took note of my surroundings. Everything lovely in our world became more beautiful and precious. I began noticing the tender beauty in the smallest of things: the smell of fresh-cut grass, the blossoming bud of a flower, an unexpected smile on the face of a stranger, or the wind in my hair when I rode the bike to the cemetery. I'd stop and stare in awe at a sunset or a rainbow in the sky, my eyes filling with tears. This new awareness gifted me with a gratitude that I chose to use to conclude my journal entries each day.

I noticed something else, too: As my capacity to be still increased, so did my empathy for others. It was as though I could sense distress emanating from another person. I'd see an old man fumbling with his billfold in the checkout lane or an older woman staring blankly at the cans of coffee in the grocery store and wonder, with an ache in my heart, if the man lived in poverty or the woman was about to cry because her late husband had loved coffee. I'd tear up, just thinking about the possibility.

My heart had not just broken; it had broken wide open.

Once I allowed for stillness, I was able to resume my daily habit of writing. After all, I am a writer by trade. I had essays and articles to work on, books to write. Even now, when I'm wrestling with an issue in my life, it helps to use a journal. In the quiet morning hours before my daughters wake, I take the time to be still, collect my thoughts, and then begin writing, contemplating, and ruminating on paper. It's amazing how that practice of expressive writing often reveals an answer to my dilemma.

Expressive writing can be a simple way to ease into the practice of "being still" for those unaccustomed to silence. Taking time for contemplative silence before you begin writing can help collect your thoughts for a more productive writing session.

Be still. The silence will eventually become
a friend. And within it, maybe we can
hear what we've never heard before.
—Stephanie Ericsson, *Companion
Through the Darkness*

Be still, and know that I am God.

—Psalm 46:10 (KJV)

God never gives us more than we can handle.
When we see each joy and, yes, each sorrow
that comes to us as a gift, and we greet both
with gratitude, that's what makes us stronger
people. That gratitude is what helps us build
our faith and gives us purpose while we're here.
Otherwise, so much would be unbearable.
—John Schlimm, *Five Years in Heaven*

When the train goes through a tunnel
and the world gets dark, do you jump
out? Of course not. You sit still and trust
the engineer to get you through.
—Corrie ten Boom

BROKEN OR BROKEN OPEN

With the death of my husband, it felt as though my heart had broken. It wasn't long before I heard my family described in the same way.

"We have help for kids like yours, from a broken home," a youth leader assured me when I'd asked him about the availability of local youth groups. I stiffened in response, ready to indignantly retort that neither my home nor my family was "broken," when I suddenly realized he was right. In an instant, I'd become a single mom, part of a statistical anomaly: children being raised without a father.

The death of a spouse affects more than the dynamics of couplehood. If there are children in the home or the financial situation has changed dramatically, the surviving spouse has additional stressors to face. Within two years of my husband's death, I would need to find employment and would go from being a mostly stay-at-home mom to one who'd spend the majority of her children's waking hours working outside the house.

That first year, my nine-year-old traveled with me to libraries all over Iowa, hanging out in the children's section while I conducted workshops. When I found employment as director of a small-town library, the library board agreed I could bring my two youngest homeschooled daughters to work with me. By the time I began working as a reporter for the local newspaper, my youngest was twelve, old enough to be left at home with her older sister.

Most days, though, I felt like I was juggling too many balls, dropping them repeatedly. It didn't lessen the single-mom guilt at all to realize I was cooking so rarely for my children that a local deli owner once prepared my regular Monday lunch before I arrived to order it.

Outside of the difficulties of navigating single parenthood, the ramifications of being "broken" aren't all negative. It is through my brokenness that I learned what it is to minister to others. I soon realized my heart hadn't just broken; it had broken *wide open*. Shortly after my husband's death, I began feeling more appreciative of others—even strangers.

The evening of David's wake, I was notified I'd won a scholarship for a writing conference that would end on what would have been our wedding anniversary. So, three months after my husband's death, I found myself in Wheaton, Illinois, attending the Write-to-Publish conference.

Normally shy, loss seemed to have given me a bravado I'd never before possessed. I found myself approaching the workshop instructors and other attendees, just to talk. On the morning of the last day, I forced myself to sit at a table full of women I didn't know. I looked around as they laughed among themselves, surprised to find myself admiring their innate beauty, the light of God shining through them. It was unlike me to see grace and beauty in strangers. When one woman asked for prayers for her roommate, the others stopped eating, taking hold of each other's hands while the one across the table from me prayed out loud. Clasped by strangers on either side of me, my hands shook slightly as I gathered courage to speak.

"Would you add me to that prayer?" I could barely talk past the lump forming in my throat. "Today would have been my thirty-third wedding anniversary. My husband died in March."

Tears streamed down my face as that group of beautiful strangers lifted me in prayer. It would be the first of many instances I would either reach out to a stranger or have one reach out to me. This was unlike my usual reticent self, the woman who'd always remained somewhat aloof in her shyness and distrust of others. I'd been bullied so badly as a child, I'd never trusted the kindness of others, particularly females. Now I was not only actively seeking human connections; I was experiencing a sort of compassion and love that would serve me well when I began doing grief presentations a year after David's death.

Through allowing others to minister to me, I learned what a gift the ministry of presence is—of simply sitting with someone in their pain. It's a lesson I wouldn't have learned without the experience of my own shattering loss. I'm a different person because of my brokenness. Now, walking through a store or dealing with the public, I remind myself daily that everyone has their own private battles, and we are all here to help each other Home.

Recording moments of compassion in my journal revealed how much I had changed. I could look back and see how ministering to others helped me too. By noting the people who crossed my path, I could clearly see when it was more than just a random encounter. A stranger could be responsible for that day's little piece of hope I'd inscribe in my journal that evening. "The cashier made me laugh today," I'd write. Or, "A former teacher saw me in the library. He came over and gave me a hug. He didn't even say anything, but the hug meant the world to me."

When we understand our own pain, we then become suffering ministers to serve others in their pain. Our own suffering is the starting point, not the impediment, of loving others through their suffering by our presence. We touch people deeply not because of our professional title but because of our personal openness.

—Barry Corey, *Love Kindness: Discover the Power of a Forgotten Christian Virtue*

The most beautiful people we have known
are those who have known defeat, known
suffering, known struggle, known loss, and
have found their way out of the depths. These
persons have an appreciation, a sensitivity, and
an understanding of life that fills them with
compassion, gentleness, and a deep loving
concern. Beautiful people do not just happen.
—Elisabeth Kübler-Ross, *Death:*
The Final Stage of Growth

Grief can be a powerful catalyst for life-enhancing change. Make the decision to search for, and uncover, at least one thing of significance emerging from your experience.
—Judy Brizendine, *Stunned By Grief*

I will never forget the moment your
heart stopped and mine kept beating.
—Angela Miller, *You Are the Mother of All Mothers*

SEEKING SUPPORT

When my husband died, I didn't know any other widows outside of my mother, who'd passed away just seventeen months before. And while my adult children, siblings, and good friends all surrounded me during those early days of mourning, they didn't know the pain of losing a spouse, leading me to feel more isolated and alone in grief.

For the first year or two after David's death, I managed to avoid attending any weddings or large gatherings, instinctively knowing they would be too much for me to handle emotionally. People seemed to understand that then, though they might be surprised to learn that kind of thing remains difficult for me, even five years later.

Family gatherings or church activities where everyone is coupled up are landmines to navigate. It would have been easy to cease attending gatherings altogether, but I knew that wasn't healthy, either. I didn't want to stay isolated, locked away by the fear of grief.

I'd already discovered that reading books by authors who'd gone down this same path was helpful. Surely being in a room among those who'd experienced a similar loss would also be. Thus, I began my search for a grief support group, a safe place to share feelings, cry, or do whatever it was people in support groups did. I wanted to be able to talk freely about my loss, certain that family and friends were tired of hearing it. More than that, I wanted encouragement from those who were further out from the loss of a spouse—to hear that the anguish I was experiencing would diminish. These were my objectives in searching for a support group.

The first two groups I tried didn't prove to be at all helpful in that regard. In one group, everyone in attendance had lost a parent, not a spouse. And while I agree that losing a parent is painful, I intimately knew that the death of a spouse was dramatically different.

The second group scared me off support groups for a long time. With widows on either side of me proclaiming that the pain would get worse in a year or three, I couldn't begin to comprehend how I'd survive if that proved true. I imagined I could actually die if the pain and anguish increased. I was also determined to never become the widow who, at five years out, was still bemoaning my loss.

Those were my only two options in our small town, so I ventured to a larger town for an evening gathering for widows and widowers. Being in a room full of people who intimately understood my particular loss was comforting, but the majority of them were well over seventy, and none had children at home like I did. Eventually, I attempted to form a support group of my own, but once again, all of the members were much older than me. While I was looking for something more in the way of spiritual support, they were looking for social support with board games, potlucks, and, evidently, the possibility of a date. It took just two separate eighty-year-old men asking me out for me to disband the group.

I needed to find my people, my clan—to seek a safe place for commiseration and spiritual and emotional support.

Thinking a Christian support group might fill that need, I tried a Bible study at a nearby church. Delving into the Bible with a group of women was helpful, but when I began working at a library, a morning study no longer worked. When I didn't immediately discover an evening group, I decided to begin one of my own. It turned out others were looking for the same thing; fifty people signed up for that first class, including a few widows and one widower.

Four years later, the Bible study has moved from a church into my home, with meetings once or twice a month. Of the eight remaining members, three have lost a spouse. This group of my own making has lifted me in ways other groups haven't. They've become like a second family to me. While we discuss our lessons and read the Bible, we often get off-topic and just talk. Even more importantly, we laugh together.

My daughter Elizabeth, who'd lost her eight-year-old son to cancer, is one of our members. One evening during a particularly rambunctious meeting, we ended up laughing so hard we cried. Elizabeth later commented, "I think that must be what heaven is like."

Despite a real need for socialization, it soon became apparent that not every group I belonged to served as a support system for me. In one, where members continually blasted their husband or ex-husband, I'd sit silently while my brain seethed, *At least you have a husband!* David and I had not had a perfect union by any means; we'd survived some pretty rough patches. Still, I would have relived even the worst moments of my marriage just for the chance to see him again.

I couldn't bear to witness the discontent of other marriages during those early days of mourning. When I realized I always left the meetings more despondent, I made the decision to remove myself from that group, at least temporarily. I needed to surround myself with positive, uplifting people.

It was the same with movies and books. I didn't want to read about a widow sucked deep down into a dark pit of despair when I was finally managing to climb out of my own. Nor did I desire movies filled with pain and darkness. Instead, it helped to watch comedies and uplifting movies or read inspirational memoirs and books about faith.

I believe it takes great courage to walk through the door of any kind of support group the first time, but when we discover the right one, it can make all the difference in our healing. Mine just happened to be a Bible study instead of a grief support group.

A journal can serve as a part of your support system in that it is a safe place to record your innermost thoughts. When it seems like everyone else has moved on beyond the loss while you're still mired in it, writing expressively can alleviate some of the loneliness. Even writing a letter to your loved one can be helpful. My journals include notes to David, prayers, and concrete goals for helping myself.

Aware of a tendency to isolate myself, I can see in my journal when I've been alone too much. I begin obsessing, becoming a bit paranoid. Those might be the times when I have to force myself to socialize, and where better to do so than in a room of people who know loss?

Writing down what you are looking for in a support group can also be helpful, serving as your guide as you test out groups.

Though it is a solitary experience we must
face alone, loss is also a common experience
that can lead us to community. It can
create a community of brokenness.
—Jerry L. Sittser, *A Grace Disguised:*
How the Soul Grows through Loss

Though we will never know how it feels
to live in someone else's loss, grief has
the capacity to connect us even across
deep divides. Fierce loss can forge fierce
connections. Grief holds the power to help
us recognize our shared fragility and also to
call forth our mutual resilience as we meet
one another in sometimes unspeakable pain.
—Jan Richardson, *The Cure for Sorrow*

We healed each other by speaking the unspeakable. In the safety of one another's company, where we would offend no one, and hurt neither ourselves nor others, we grieved— something not allowed in the world at large.
—Stephanie Ericsson, *Companion Through the Darkness*

There is no path so dark, nor road so steep,
nor hill so slippery that other people have
not been there before me and survived.
May my dark times teach me to help the
people I love on similar journeys.
—Maggie Bedrosian

SEEING THE LIGHT

For more than a year after my husband died, my friend Mary would travel eighty miles once a month to visit me. She'd treat me to lunch at a tearoom, and we'd talk for hours. Mostly, I talked while she listened. Before she'd leave for home, we'd walk down the alley to my sister's consignment store. Nearly every visit, Mary would leave the store with a table lamp in her hands, until it got to be almost ridiculous how many she was carting home.

Mary's husband questioned the frequent purchases, and she really couldn't really explain the compulsion at the time. In her letters following the newest acquisition, she'd mention the glow of a nearby lamp. And then another. It wasn't long before every corner of her house was lit by a soft glow.

Only later, when the lamp-buying binge ceased, would Mary and I consider how the purchases might have served as a coping mechanism for a woman who was companioning her friend through one of the darkest periods of her life.

I, on the other hand, was just purchasing too much stuff in general—pillows, wall hangings, decorative wall plaques, stationery, and books—searching desperately for that one possession that might fill the gaping wound in my heart. My closet was filling up, too, with jewelry, scarves, and bright-colored clothing. Most things were secondhand or from a clearance rack, but the purchases still added up. But no matter how much I bought, nothing alleviated the pain or filled that awful hole in my heart.

Financially, the buying binges were unhealthy, but my urge to surround myself with beauty and inspirational messages was not. Many of those items from that period of buying remain in my home today: a butterfly pillow, inspirational plaques, and pictures on my walls.

Author Alexandra Stoddard is convinced that our surroundings can nourish us physically, emotionally, and spiritually. "Our home is the only place on earth we have control over. We're free to paint our bathroom ceiling sky blue and turn our rooms into gardens, beaches, woods and conservatories," she wrote in *Choosing Happiness*. "Within the privacy of our walls, we're free to create the most joyful environment that enlarges our love of life, cultivates and inspires us to celebrate life in the modest rhythms of the everyday."

Possessions aren't all bad. Our desire to surround ourselves with beautiful things (or, in the case of my friend Mary, light) is natural. Fresh flowers on the table, a wall plaque with an inspirational message, or the soft glow of a lamp in the corner of the room can be soothing to the soul. There are many things in my home that bring me joy, particularly in my home office. My favorites are handmade, like my mother's wood carvings, artwork, painted brick books, and wooden letters spelling out the word *WRITE* with the cover designs of my books, all crafted by creative daughters. My book lamp, a handmade quilt on a trunk, and solid oak bookcases filled with books—these things make me feel as though I am surrounded by warmth and beauty.

My morning ritual begins in my office each day, sitting in a recliner with a cup of coffee nearby. I'm never sure if it's the surroundings, the gift of silence, or the caffeine that jump-starts my day. It might be a combination of the three. But it is in this space—this haven—that my best writing comes.

While I chose to surround myself with inspiring messages in the form of wall hangings and plaques, that might not be your style. I have seven different such "messages" in my office alone, an excess in the opinion of my daughters. I've heard of people who simply tape an inspirational quote or pertinent Bible verse to their bathroom mirror.

My journal pages are filled with inspirational quotes and meaningful passages from books. Occasionally, I'll flip through the pages of previous journals, searching for something to lift my spirits. Inscribing other people's words in a journal can be a jumping-off point for your own expressive writing.

And while I'm not suggesting that you go crazy spending money to renovate or refurbish your house, I do see the immense value in bringing cheerful, colorful things into your home or writing space. Surrounding yourself in light can help pierce the fog that so often comes with grief.

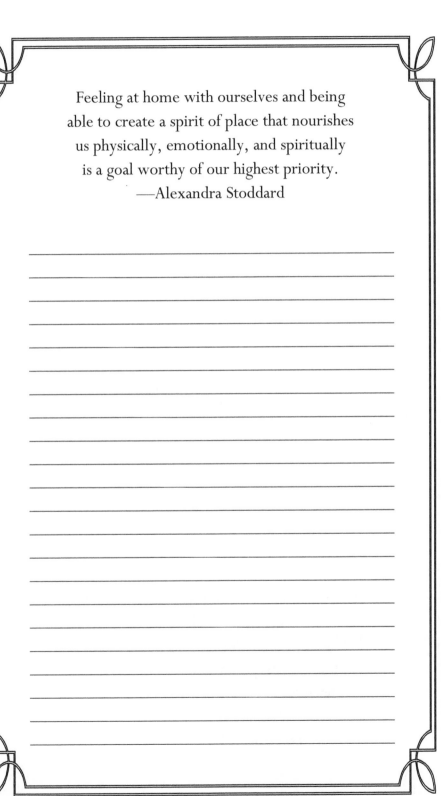

Feeling at home with ourselves and being
able to create a spirit of place that nourishes
us physically, emotionally, and spiritually
is a goal worthy of our highest priority.
—Alexandra Stoddard

Instead, I have learned things in the dark that
I could never have learned in the light, things
that have saved my life over and over again, so
that there is really only one logical conclusion.
I need darkness as much as I need light.
—Barbara Brown Taylor,
Learning to Walk in the Dark

The friend who can be silent with us in a moment of despair or confusion, who can stay with us in an hour of grief and bereavement, who can tolerate not knowing, not curing, not healing and face with us the reality of our powerlessness, that is a friend who cares.
—Henri Nouwen, *Out of Solitude*

_____

_____

_____

_____

_____

_____

_____

_____

_____

_____

_____

_____

_____

_____

_____

_____

_____

_____

_____

_____

_____

_____

Trusting God when the miracle does not come,
when the urgent prayer gets no answer, when
there is only darkness—this is the kind of faith
God values perhaps most of all. This is the kind
of faith that can be developed and displayed
only in the midst of difficult circumstances.
This is the kind of faith that cannot be shaken
because it is the result of having been shaken.
—Nancy Guthrie, *Holding On to Hope*

HOLIDAYS AND OTHER HURDLES

Eight months after my husband's death, I thought I was handling things well. Then the holiday season hit. I'd gotten through the first Easter, our wedding anniversary, and both our youngest child's birthday and my own—all without David. Surely the first Thanksgiving and Christmas couldn't be much worse.

But they were, especially Christmas.

David had once dubbed me the "Queen of Christmas." I'd purchase gifts year-round, make cutout sugar cookies, fill stockings, and wrap dozens of gifts for each of our eight children. Then, no matter how little sleep I'd gotten the night before, I'd be up before dawn with the excitement of seeing our children's faces as they trooped down the stairs and caught sight of the bounty of gifts underneath the tree.

The year David died, I had no desire to celebrate holidays at all, but I had a nine-year-old and seven other children to consider, so I made a valiant attempt. I didn't fare well that first Christmas. I couldn't even manage to put up our usual artificial tree and ornaments. Instead, I purchased a pre-lit tree online and had it delivered to my door. And while I made cutout sugar cookies, purchased and wrapped gifts, and filled the children's stockings, I forgot to cook the traditional spiral ham. In fact, I forgot all about dinner and had to drive to a gas station for frozen pizza.

Getting through the holidays or special anniversary dates can be difficult. The following suggestions stem both from personal experience and from talking to others who have shared their own stories about what they found helpful:

Grief Is Heightened During Holidays, Anniversaries, and Special Days

That's a fact. Forewarned is forearmed. It's a normal reaction to miss a family member or loved one even more on special days. The first holiday season, especially, is a milestone hurdle. Consider marking the occasion or honoring your loved one's memory in some way. It might be making a monetary donation in their name. It could be a ritual of some sort, like releasing a balloon to the sky or purchasing a special tree ornament. Some people find it helpful to donate their time by ringing the Salvation Army bell, serving food to the homeless, or volunteering at a shelter.

Despite my expectations for that first-year anniversary of my husband's death, I was surprised to discover that the anticipation of it was much worse than the experience of the actual day itself. That might be because I had planned for it by marking the day with my first-ever pedicure (complete with a butterfly on my big toe) and lunch with my sisters. Or it could be that dreading something for so long made the reality of it mild by comparison. Whatever the case, I can honestly say I survived that milestone day without too much emotional damage.

Do Whatever It Takes to Get Through the Holidays

My children and I did something unprecedented in the Kenyon family the first Thanksgiving without their dad: We went out to eat at a buffet-style restaurant. In contrast, a widower I know found comfort in keeping everything exactly the same for the holidays. He hired someone to clean the house and bake cookies, then invited his children over for Christmas Day. His daughters made the traditional Christmas meal that their mother had always cooked.

The first Christmas without my grandson Jacob was going to be excruciating, but my daughter Elizabeth had three other children to consider. It was one of them who came up with the idea of exchanging "ugly" gifts and seeing who could find the most hideous one. It was the first time I had seen a light in Elizabeth's eyes since her son's death, so I welcomed the idea. She and I vied for the most hideous gift for several weeks, teasing each other with hints about the amazing finds we were discovering. I keep the ugly, misshapen sheep candle she found for me displayed inside a glass cabinet as a reminder of how something simple, or even a bit silly, can pull us out of misery for a short while.

Don't Just Grieve; Do Something!

With loss, emotional pain is inevitable. Will you waste your pain by allowing it to close you off to others or utilize it by opening up your heart to help others?

When I discovered my mother's address book among her things after her death, an inkling of an idea formed. She'd fully expected to see another Christmas after undergoing radiation, and I decided to use a box of Christmas cards she had stashed away and utilize her address book to send cards to everyone in it, including many who might not have heard about her early-November death. It wasn't an entirely altruistic move; it helped me reach out to people Mom had cared about, and I heard back from many of them.

Because my husband died on a Tuesday morning, I began dreading Tuesdays, hating the weekday reminder of my loss. I couldn't help but do the count: two weeks without David, three weeks without David, four weeks without David . . . until I got sick and tired of it. I couldn't hate Tuesdays for the rest of my life. I decided to do something outside of myself every Tuesday by writing out cards or letters to someone on that day. I followed that Tuesday-morning ritual for more than three years. Even now, I look forward to Tuesdays, making an effort to reach out to someone, even if I might not get to the task until Wednesday or Thursday. Part of the fun is anticipating each week who will be the recipient. I never expect anything in return, so I am pleasantly surprised when someone writes me back to tell me the card reached them just when they needed it most.

After my grandson Jacob died, my daughter and I designed Random Acts of Kindness cards that we utilize in his honor. We might pay for the person behind us in line at a fast-food place, leaving the card behind, or we might buy a piece of pie for an old man sitting alone in a restaurant. My grandchildren came up with some wonderful ideas of their own: taping a plastic baggie with a dollar and a Jacob Random Act of Kindness card in it on a pop machine or leaving three quarters and a card near the carwash vacuum.

Look at it another way: Grief can free us to do things differently and to celebrate the holidays in quieter, more meaningful ways. As the Queen of Christmas, I'd built up a huge amount of stress, attempting to pull together a bigger and better Christmas every year. I was no longer enjoying myself. Despite purchasing gifts year-round, by Thanksgiving I was scrambling to fill in the obvious holes so that one child wouldn't be getting more than another.

Post-grief, I could finally abandon some of the duties and rituals of Christmas I didn't particularly care for, like baking Christmas cookies or putting up the tree. I had daughters who were more than willing to take over some of the tasks I'd micromanaged for over thirty years. Holding down a job outside of the house, I was no longer capable of doing everything or spending an entire year searching for the perfect gifts. I lightened up on the gift-purchasing, but it was time to do so anyway. My gift-buying had gotten out of control, and the role of Queen of Christmas had already become a burden, so I welcomed the changes.

Remember Past Holidays and Record Little Celebrations

When the grief threatens to overwhelm you during the holidays, try shifting your focus by utilizing your journal to write about the last Christmas you spent with your loved one or about a favorite anniversary memory. Record your gratitude for all the amazing moments with which you were blessed. I had over thirty years with David, and those memories, celebrations, and joys come back to comfort and strengthen me when the emotional hurdles threaten to overwhelm me.

Oh, if only someone had prepared me for a setback on anniversaries. Anniversaries of births, deaths, special moments, dreadful times, triumphant victories can exhume past pain as if it were fresh.
—Stephanie Ericsson, *Companion Through the Darkness*

_____

_____

_____

_____

_____

_____

_____

_____

_____

_____

_____

_____

_____

_____

_____

_____

_____

_____

"You have no idea how well you are doing,"
John complimented me just a few minutes after
he mentioned the Christmas card. What did
that mean: That I was doing well? That I'd come
to a family gathering? That I'd remembered to
bring food? That I was dressed, and my hair,
combed? That I was wearing shoes? I wasn't
sure, but maybe just making an appearance at a
family event meant I was handling things well.
—Mary Potter Kenyon, *Refined By
Fire: A Journey of Grief and Grace*

Grief is a tidal wave that overtakes you, smashes down upon you with unimaginable force, sweeps you up into its darkness, where you tumble and crash against unidentifiable surfaces, only to be thrown out on an unknown beach, bruised, reshaped. . . . Grief will make a new person out of you, if it doesn't kill you in the making.
—Stephanie Ericsson, *Companion Through the Darkness*

Now there are spaces in the mind, spaces in the days and night. Often, when we least expect it, the pain and the preoccupation come back and back—sometimes like the toiling crash of an ocean wave, sometimes like the slow ooze after a piece of driftwood is lifted and water and sand rise to claim their own once more.

—Martha Hickman, *Healing After Loss*

GLIMPSES OF GROWTH

The summer after I graduated from high school, I lived with my brother and his wife in Cedar Falls, where I'd be attending college that fall. I met David at the restaurant where I worked as a waitress. We began dating in July. In August, I moved into the dorm with an assigned roommate I didn't know. I spent the majority of my time with my new boyfriend. We got married the following summer. I gave birth to the first of my eight children when I was just twenty years old. By the time David died in 2012, I'd been someone's wife for almost thirty-three years—nearly all of my adult life. I barely knew who I was without him.

It might seem odd to write about finding joy and purpose in a journal designed for those who grieve, but when I look at my journals from the year following my husband's death, I notice a pattern. While I was certainly reading dozens of books about grief and bereavement, I was also picking up books about heaven, creativity, and following our talents and passions. Books about heaven reassured me I would see David again. The books on creativity and discovering our purpose in life helped me just as much, in a different way. I was actively seeking meaning from my loss and purpose in my life. I needed to find out who I was outside of being a wife.

In an effort to build up my author platform and make a little extra money, I'd started doing writing and couponing workshops in the fall of 2011. David would drive me to my destinations, claiming the time alone with me in the car more than made up for the wait while I conducted the workshop.

Just two months before his death, he drove me to a photo shoot for a weekly newspaper column I had been hired to write. On the way home from the appointment, we'd laughed over the incredulity of it all: me, at a photo shoot! In the next instant, he predicted that the workshops and the newspaper column were just the beginning for me. He'd been the one to encourage me to write both the couponing book I'd been attempting to sell for two years and another one on caregiving that I'd stashed in a file cabinet after pitching to eighty-eight agents. He believed both books would be published someday.

"You're flying," David told me in the car that day, obviously pleased. "This is your time to soar."

David wouldn't live to see either of those books published. I signed a contract for the couponing book seven months after his death. Less than a year later, I sold the caregiving one. I would go on to sign three more book contracts in the next three years.

David had been right. Those initial classes and the weekly newspaper column were just the beginning for me. Besides the book contracts, I branched out from community college workshops to present at libraries, book stores, and writer's conferences. I eventually got a job as a newspaper reporter.

But it was David's faith in me and the subsequent loss of him that was behind my foray into public speaking. Approximately one year after his death, I stood in front of three separate church congregations to share my story of loss, my search for something to hold on to, and my journey of faith. As I spoke from the heart, I noticed people in each of the churches wiping away tears.

I'd been writing for more than thirty years, and I'd known that written words could make a difference in other people's lives. But for the first time, I realized the full power of the *spoken* word.

It wasn't long before someone who'd heard me speak asked me to address their church group on a similar topic. Then someone else asked the same thing. Soon, I'd added public speaking to my roster. It was after I spoke before a roomful of grieving people that I realized I never felt more alive than when I was speaking in front of an audience. I'd discovered a new talent and passion.

I was experiencing many other "firsts" in my new life without David. While David had driven me everywhere during our marriage, thanks to a GPS from my son and the need to travel to workshops all over Iowa, I gained confidence in my own driving ability. I also got on an airplane for the first time and attended a concert, both experiences my husband had vowed to share with me "someday."

There was a bittersweet sadness to seeing the book my husband had believed in filling the window of a Barnes & Noble bookstore. How could I enjoy the experience when the man behind the book wasn't there to see it? Or looking out the window and seeing the clouds during my first plane ride. Or sitting in a concert hall for the first time. David was supposed to be there! What about welcoming a new granddaughter or witnessing both a son and daughter getting married?

According to his published diaries, Charles Lutwidge Dodgson, better known as author Lewis Carroll, marked special days as "white-stone days" in his journal. Since David's death, I mark white-stone *moments* in mine—sweet moments I will remember forever, that I wish he were here to share.

Despite the twinge of sadness that accompanies my white-stone moments, I treasure each one and look forward to more of them.

Gifts of grace come to all of us. But we must be
ready to see and willing to receive these gifts.
It will require a kind of sacrifice, the sacrifice
of believing that, however painful our losses,
life can still be good—good in a different way
than before, but nevertheless good. I will never
recover from my loss and I will never get over
missing the ones I lost. But I still cherish life . . .
—Jerry L. Sittser, *A Grace Disguised:*
How the Soul Grows through Loss

Sometimes the best way for us to get
inner direction is not to seek it. To
stop trying to solve the problem and
allow God to whisper a solution.

—Cecil Murphey, *Making Sense When Life Doesn't*

I have been trying to make the best of
grief and am just beginning to learn to
allow it to make the best of me.
—Barbara Lazear Ascher

"For I know the plans I have for you," declares
the Lord, "plans to prosper you and not to harm
you, plans to give you hope and a future."
—Jeremiah 29:11 (NIV)

MARKING MILESTONES

Recently, someone newly widowed asked me what it felt like, more than five years out from the loss of my spouse. I hesitated, not sure how to respond. I knew what they wanted to hear: that everything was fine, and grieving was over. What could I say that would convey truth but not alarm her?

For the most part, I'm doing fine, navigating single motherhood the best that I can, failing miserably on occasion. I have a fulfilling part-time job at a library. I enjoy public speaking and conducting writing workshops and have met my dream of having several books published.

But the truth is, there are still moments when the sharp pain of grief rises close to the surface; when a daughter gets married without her dad to walk her down the aisle or the single sob that escapes when a certain song comes on the radio. Grief can rear its ugly head with jealousy at another couple's anniversary trip or the sight of an elderly couple holding hands. It can blindside, with no warning at all.

The most accurate way to describe it is that seasoned grief *looks* and *feels* different than that dark despair of early mourning, yet remains a heavy burden. Though the heaviness of it has receded with time, the cloak of it still rests solidly on my shoulders. Grieving is lonely. It never truly ends, and only those who are intimately acquainted with it can begin to understand its depths.

Even today, more than five years after David's death, the absence of one person is keenly felt. I want so badly to share with David what I am feeling, what losing him has been like. Because we talked about everything. And nothing. And when we weren't talking, we could sit silently, holding hands.

The progression is marked clearly in my journals. In that first year, I filled two journals with grieving words. I wrote daily, searching for meaning and peace. Now, though not nearly as prolific, I still utilize expressive writing to work my way through life's tough moments.

Grief, five years out, remains a quiet, unwelcome companion.

Time passes and I am still not through it. Grief isn't something you get over. You live with it. You go on with it lodged in you. Sometimes I feel like I have swallowed a pile of stones. Grief makes me heavy. It makes me slow. Even on days when I laugh a lot, or dance, or finish a project, or meet a deadline, or celebrate, or make love, it is there. Lodged deep inside me. Time has passed and I am living a life again, back in the world.

—Ann Hood, *Comfort: A Journey Through Grief*

Healing is not a cure; no cure exists for grief.
Healing doesn't mean painless. The pain of
grief never really goes away. Healing doesn't
mean forgetting. A loved one will stay in
the heart forever. Healing means facing the
future with acceptance, gratitude, and hope.
—Margaret Brownley, *Grieving God's Way*

The reality is that you will grieve forever. You will not "get over" the loss of a loved one; you will learn to live with it. You will heal and you will rebuild yourself around the loss you have suffered. You will be whole again, but you will never be the same. Nor should you be the same, nor would you want to.

—Elisabeth Kübler-Ross and David Kessler, *On Grief and Grieving*

Suffice it to say that I now know that death
and loss can be our greatest teachers. They're
our greatest teachers because, in tearing
away the people, the possessions, the hopes
and dreams we all cling to, they offer us the
opportunity to find out who we really are,
to discover the depths of our beings . . .
—John Welshons, *Awakening from Grief*

CLIMBING OUT OF
THE PIT

For six months, the downstairs hallway remained dark. It had been even longer for the upstairs hallway. Changing lightbulbs was something my husband had always taken care of, and for whatever reason, I hadn't bothered to replace them or asked my sons to perform the simple chore. Nor had I mentioned it to my two youngest daughters, who still lived with me. Instead, we learned to work around the darkness. I'd leave the upstairs bathroom light on in the evening so we could find our way up the otherwise darkened stairwell, and if we needed something out of the downstairs closet, we'd just prop open the bathroom door across that hallway and turn on the light to illuminate the dark depths of the closet. In other words, we adapted to the darkness.

Then, during one of her visits, my older daughter Rachel offered to help me clean out a cabinet I hadn't touched since her dad's death. While transferring some things to the hallway closet, she asked why the light switch wasn't working. When I sheepishly admitted that it wasn't the switches but the lightbulbs, her younger sister, Katie, gasped in astonishment.

"You mean all this time the hallway lights worked, and you just needed to replace the lightbulbs? Why didn't you tell me? I thought they were broken."

I mumbled something about a fear of falling off ladders, but the truth was, I had no real explanation as to why I hadn't changed the lightbulbs.

Within minutes, my two daughters had located the ladder and climbed up to replace both bulbs. When they flipped the switches on, the hallways were illuminated with brightness for the first time in months. We no longer had to live in the shadows.

The first year of widowhood was much the same for me. With the death of my husband, a light inside of me had gone out. It was as if I'd lost all joy. The reality was that I got used to living that way. For a long time, the fog of grief permeated everything. I felt wrapped in a cloak of sadness. I'd wonder if I'd ever truly feel joy again. Just as the bathroom light illuminated the dark closet, there were those brief moments when I'd catch a glimpse of brightness. But for the most part, I adjusted to living in the dark night of the soul.

Like the simple lightbulb I'd put off replacing, I discovered there were things I could do to bring light back into my life. Allowing for contemplative silence and prayer helped. So did reading devotionals or books written by those who had gone down the grief road before me. Finding a support system in a Bible study was important and so was writing and journaling. It wasn't just any one of these things but a combination of all of them that brought me to a place of healing five years out.

Representing just how far I've come, a few weeks later it was *I* who climbed the ladder to change the smoke alarm battery that had begun beeping.

I'd had access to the lightbulbs, or the tools of healing, all along. We all do. We just have to discover what works best for us. My hope is that those who have written their way through this journal will have found some healing of their own.

Q. How many widows does it take to change a lightbulb?

A. One. It just takes one widow, but she needs to make the effort to get out the ladder and find the courage to climb to the top of it. Or find someone willing to help her.

Optional Writing Prompts

- Everyone has a story to tell. What's yours? It is in the telling that healing comes, but some find it too painful to talk about. Or maybe you have talked about the moment when your life changed, but now you feel like others are tired of hearing it. Whatever the case may be, this journal is a safe place to write your story.
- It might feel like a stretch early on in your mourning, but can you think of things you are grateful for? Make a gratitude list.
- Not only do we grieve the person who is missing from our life, but we also find we are grieving the future life we'd imagined having with them. What future are you grieving today?
- There are bound to be regrets and "if onlys" when a loved one dies. Make a list of your regrets. Now, how would your loved one respond to each of those regrets? Write down their imagined response.
- Are there things you wish you'd said to your loved one? Write them a letter.
- Writing down what you are looking for in a support group can be helpful, if you are searching for a support system. Make a list of what kind of support you need. This can serve as your guide as you test support groups.
- Sometimes, the death of a loved one can give us a different perspective on our own mortality. Make a "bucket list" of things you want to do in your life. Then check them off as you do them, even if it takes years to do them all.
- Are there books that have helped you through loss? Books you want to read? Make a list that you can refer to later or recommend to others.

- Plan ahead for those dreaded anniversaries and holidays. Is there something you can do in honor of the person you loved? A new ritual you'd like to incorporate into your celebrations? Jot down some ideas.
- Remember how author Lewis Carroll marked never-to-be-forgotten days in his journal as "white-stone" days? What are the white-stone memories you shared with your loved one? Have you experienced some white-stone days since their death? Write them down.
- Our unmet expectations can get us into trouble some days, causing undue stress and anxiety. Are there people in your life who have let you down in their response to your grief? Did you expect a type of support you didn't get? I was surprised at how little food was brought to my home, outside of sweets, during the early days of grieving, having always heard about the casseroles and meals people received after a death in the family. Write about your unmet expectations. Now ask yourself if you would have known what to do for a family before you experienced your own loss.
- Conversely, did you receive support from an unexpected source? A young girl took the time to write out pages of Bible verses for me, pages I kept in my journal for years. A youth leader from a church that wasn't my own prayed with me. A cashier at the grocery store, who barely knew me, put her hand on mine and said she was sorry. I wrote all these incidents in my journal, marveling at the kindness of strangers. Write down some of the unexpected sources of light you saw in the darkness of grief.
- You don't have to be a writer to express yourself through writing. When the writing is for ourselves and not for publication, there are no rules. Try writing a

poem about your grief. Free verse doesn't have to rhyme, nor does it have to follow a certain format.

- C. S. Lewis said, "No one ever told me that grief felt so like fear." Do you have fears about your future without the person you loved? What are they?

- We can't predict when a wave of grief might assail us. Have you had an unexpected griefburst? If so, share that on these pages. Maybe someday you will look back and laugh at the incident. Three years later, I can only imagine what the dental assistant might have thought of the woman who sobbed uncontrollably in the exam room. I was so embarrassed then, I changed dentists, but now I can laugh. Laughter can be a balm to the soul.

- What have you learned about yourself in facing loss? Maybe you are stronger, or weaker, than you ever imagined.

- Depending on how far out you are from the loss, can you feel or see (from the pages of your journal) the difference? How would you encourage someone who is newly bereaved?

- You are going to feel emotional pain after the death of a loved one. That is a given. The question is, What are you going to do with that pain? Will you use it to propel you to make changes in your life, to become a better person, or to reach out to others? Or will you waste it by wallowing in pain? Write down some ways you can utilize your pain.

Suggested Books

Choose Joy: Finding Hope and Purpose When Life Hurts by Sara Frankl and Mary Carver

Choosing Happiness: Keys to a Joyful Life by Alexandra Stoddard

Colors of Goodbye: A Memoir of Holding On, Letting Go, and Reclaiming Joy in the Wake of Loss by September Vaudrey

Comfort: A Journey Through Grief by Ann Hood

Companion Through the Darkness: Inner Dialogues on Grief by Stephanie Ericsson

The Cure for Sorrow: A Book of Blessings for Times of Grief by Jan Richardson

Five Years in Heaven: The Unlikely Friendship That Answered Life's Greatest Questions by John Schlimm

Fly a Little Higher: How God Answered a Mom's Small Prayer in a Big Way by Laura Sobiech

Getting to the Other Side of Grief: Overcoming the Loss of a Spouse by Susan J. Zonnebelt-Smeenge and Robert C. De Vries

Grace for the Moment Morning and Evening Edition: Inspiration for Each Day of the Year by Max Lucado

A Grace Disguised: How the Soul Grows through Loss by Jerry L. Sittser

A Grief Observed by C. S. Lewis

Grief Diaries: Surviving Loss of a Spouse by Lynda Cheldelin Fell, with others

Grief Diaries: Poetry & Prose and More by Lynda Cheldelin Fell, Mary Potter Kenyon, and Marilyn Rollins

Grieving God's Way: The Path to Lasting Hope and Healing by Margaret Brownley

Heartbroken: Healing from the Loss of a Spouse by Gary Roe

Help, Thanks, Wow: The Three Essential Prayers by Anne Lamott

Healing After Loss: Daily Meditations for Working Through Grief by Martha Hickman

The Joy Diet: 10 Daily Practices for a Happier Life by Martha Beck

Knowing God, Knowing Myself: An Invitation to Daily Discovery by Cecil Murphey

Letters to My Son: Turning Loss into Legacy by Mitch Carmody

Life is Goodbye, Life is Hello: Grieving Well Through All Kinds of Loss by Dr. Alla Renée Bozarth

Love Kindness: Discover the Power of a Forgotten Christian Virtue by Barry Corey

Making Sense When Life Doesn't: The Secrets of Thriving in Tough Times by Cecil Murphey

Mary & Me: A Lasting Link Through Ink by Mary Potter Kenyon and Mary Jedlicka Humston

Motherless Daughters: The Legacy of Loss by Hope Edelman

Mourning Song by Joyce Landorf Heatherley

NIV Hope in the Mourning Bible edited by Timothy Beals

On Grief and Grieving: Finding the Meaning of Grief Through the Five Stages of Loss by Elisabeth Kübler-Ross and David Kessler

The One Year Book of Hope by Nancy Guthrie

Opening Up by Writing It Down: How Expressive Writing Improves Health and Eases Emotional Pain by Drs. James W. Pennebaker and Joshua M. Smyth

The Other Side of Sadness: What the New Science of Bereavement Tells Us About Life After Loss by George A. Bonanno

Out of Solitude: Three Meditations on the Christian Life by Henri Nouwen

Out of the Ashes: Healing in the Afterloss by Benjamin Scott Allen

Please Be Patient, I'm Grieving by Gary Roe

Refined By Fire: A Journey of Grief and Grace by Mary Potter Kenyon

Reflections of a Grieving Spouse: The Unexpected Journey from Loss to Renewed Hope by H. Norman Wright

Saying Goodbye: Facing the Loss of a Loved One by Cecil Murphey and Gary Roe

Stunned By Grief: Remapping Your Life When Loss Changes Everything by Judy Brizendine

The Truth About Grief: The Myth of Its Five Stages and the New Science of Loss by Ruth Davis Konigsberg

Turn My Mourning into Dancing: Finding Hope in Hard Times by Henri Nouwen

Two-Part Invention: The Story of a Marriage by Madeleine L'Engle

Understanding Your Grief: Ten Essential Touchstones for Finding Hope and Healing Your Heart by Dr. Alan D. Wolfelt

When Your Soulmate Dies: A Guide to Healing Through Heroic Mourning by Alan D. Wolfelt

Writing as a Way of Healing: How Telling Our Stories Transforms Our Lives by Louise DeSalvo

The Year of Magical Thinking by Joan Didion

You Are the Mother of All Mothers by Angela Miller

Suggested Websites

The Compassionate Friends

www.compassionatefriends.com
The Compassionate Friends nonprofit organization exists to provide friendship, understanding, and hope to those going through the natural grieving process.

Faith & Grief

www.faithandgrief.org
A ministry of compassion and connection; includes daily devotionals, stories of grief, and healing resources.

Grief Diaries

www.griefdiaries.com
Village of people helping people; includes a series of books written by the true experts—those who have experienced loss. Healing hearts by sharing journeys.

Grief.com

www.grief.com
David Kessler, an author and expert on grieving, shares resources for those who grieve and those who want to help them.

GriefNet

www.griefnet.org
Internet community of people dealing with grief, death, and major loss; offers fifty email support groups, including support groups for adults and children.

GriefShare

www.griefshare.org
Grief recovery support group; includes online, email, and in-person support.

The Grief Toolbox

www.grieftoolbox.com
Resources and tools to help grievers, with a marketplace for purchasing books.

Hospice Foundation of America

www.hospicefoundation.org
End-of-life resources, along with information about grief support.

Open to Hope

www.opentohope.com
Nonprofit foundation with the mission of helping people find hope after loss.

A Widow's Might

www.anewseason.net
Online retreat for grieving widows and Christian devotions for women.

ABOUT THE AUTHOR

MARY POTTER KENYON graduated from the University of Northern Iowa with a BA in psychology and is a certified grief counselor. By day, she works as Senior Services librarian for the James Kennedy Public Library. By night, she is a public speaker, grief support group leader, and writing instructor for community colleges. She is widely published in newspapers, magazines, and anthologies. Several of her devotions were featured in the 2013 *Hope in the Mourning* Bible. Mary is the author of four previous Familius titles, including the award-winning *Refined By Fire: A Journey of Grief and Grace*. She lives in Manchester, Iowa, with two of her eight children. Visit her website at www.marypotterkenyon.com.

ABOUT FAMILIUS

Visit Our Website: www.familius.com

Join Our Family

There are lots of ways to connect with us! Subscribe to our news-letters at www.familius.com to receive uplifting daily inspiration, essays from our Pater Familius, a free ebook every month, and the first word on special discounts and Familius news.

Get Bulk Discounts

If you feel a few friends and family might benefit from what you've read, let us know and we'll be happy to provide you with quantity discounts. Simply email us at orders@familius.com.

Connect

Facebook: www.facebook.com/paterfamilius
Twitter: @familiustalk, @paterfamilius1
Pinterest: www.pinterest.com/familius
Instagram: @familiustalk

FAMILIUS

The most important work you ever do will be within the walls of your own home.

CPSIA information can be obtained
at www.ICGtesting.com
Printed in the USA
BVHW082221130320
575013BV00001B/6